THE STORY BEHIND
JUNETEENTH

JACK READER

PowerKiDS
press.

New York

Published in 2020 by The Rosen Publishing Group, Inc.
29 East 21st Street, New York, NY 10010

First Edition

Editor: Tanya Dellaccio
Book Design: Reann Nye

Photo Credits: Cover, p. 1 Bastiaan Slabbers/iStock Photo; pp. 4, 6, 8, 10, 12, 14, 16, 18, 20, 22 (background) Preto Perola/Shutterstock.com; pp. 5, 22 Kathryn Scott Osler/Denver Post/Getty Images; p. 7 UniversalImagesGroup/Getty Images; p. 9 https://en.wikipedia.org/wiki/File:Chickamauga.jpg; p.11 https://commons.wikimedia.org/wiki/File:Emancipation_proclamation.jpg; pp. 13, 19 Everett Historical/Shutterstock.com; p. 15 Rawpixel.com/Shutterstock.com; p. 17 DEA/BIBLIOTECA AMBROSIANA/De Agostini/Getty Images; p. 21 Bettmann/Getty Images; p. 22 Kathryn Scott Osler/Denver Post/Getty Images.

Cataloging-in-Publication Data

Names: Reader, Jack.
Title: The story behind Juneteenth / Jack Reader.
Description: New York : PowerKids Press, 2020. | Series: Holiday Histories | Includes glossary and index.
Identifiers: ISBN 9781725300521 (pbk.) | ISBN 9781725300545 (library bound) | ISBN 9781725300538 (6pack)
Subjects: LCSH: Juneteenth–Juvenile literature. | Slaves–Emancipation–Texas–Juvenile literature. | African Americans–Anniversaries, etc.–Juvenile literature. | African Americans–Social life and customs–Juvenile literature.
Classification: LCC E185.93.T4 R43 2020 | DDC 394.263–dc23

Manufactured in the United States of America

CPSIA Compliance Information: Batch #CSPK19. For Further Information contact Rosen Publishing, New York, New York at 1-800-237-9932.

CONTENTS

June 19 4

Slavery in the United States . . . 6

The Emancipation
    Proclamation 10

Juneteenth! 12

A Forgotten Holiday 16

Celebrating Freedom 20

On the Rise 22

Glossary 23

Index 24

Websites 24

June 19

Juneteenth—June 19—is a very important day. It marks the end of **slavery** in the United States. For a long time, not many people **celebrated** this historic holiday. It's only recently that more people have started to remember and celebrate Juneteenth again.

Slavery in the United States

Ship captains first brought African slaves to North America in the early 1600s. Many slaves were forced to work on large farms in the South. By the 1700s, many people began realizing slavery was bad. By 1804, all the northern states had started to end slavery.

Many people in the North and the South didn't agree about slavery. As more states joined the United States, more people became **divided** on the issue. The **Civil War** began in 1861 because of the disagreements between the North and the South.

The Emancipation Proclamation

President Abraham Lincoln's goal was to keep the United States together. In time, he decided that freeing the slaves would help this goal. In 1863, he issued the Emancipation Proclamation, which freed all slaves in states controlled by the South. Still, this couldn't be **enforced** in many places.

11

Juneteenth!

News of the Emancipation Proclamation spread slowly through the South. In April 1865, the North won the Civil War. Two months later, African Americans in Texas learned about the proclamation. When they did—on June 19, 1865—they celebrated their freedom.

13

Former slaves and others celebrated Juneteenth (which is short for June 19th) for the first time in 1866. Celebrations soon spread to other states. **Traditions**, including praying, singing, and wearing new clothes to mark their freedom, soon became part of the holiday for many African Americans. People continue these traditions today!

A Forgotten Holiday

Even though many African Americans celebrated Juneteenth during the late 1800s, it never became an official holiday in the United States. The years after the Civil War were hard for states in the South. Few people in power were interested in celebrating the end of slavery.

After the war, people disagreed on what to do about former slaves and former slave states. During the early and mid-1900s, white people made many laws to enforce **segregation**. Former slaves had been freed, but African Americans still had little freedom. Many people forgot about Juneteenth and its meaning.

REX
THEATRE
FOR COLORED PEOPLE

19

Celebrating Freedom

During the 1950s and 1960s, the civil rights movement was growing, and segregation started being banned throughout the United States. African Americans began celebrating their freedom again. In 1980, Texas became the first state to make Juneteenth an official holiday.

21

On the Rise

Today, Juneteenth celebrations are on the rise again. Washington, D.C., and 39 states now mark the day, though few have made it an official holiday. Still, people across the United States gather on June 19 to pray, sing, dance, and share the history of the day slavery finally ended.

GLOSSARY

celebrate: To do something special or enjoyable for an important event or holiday.

Civil War: A war fought from 1861 to 1865 between the North and the South in the United States over slavery and other issues.

divided: Split.

enforce: To make sure that people do what is required by law.

segregation: The separation of people based on race, class, or ethnicity.

slavery: The state of being a slave and the practice of owning slaves, or people who are "owned" by another person and are forced to work for that person without pay.

tradition: A way of thinking, behaving, or doing something that's been used by people in a particular society for a long time.

INDEX

C
civil rights movement, 20
Civil War, 8, 12, 16, 18

E
Emancipation
    Proclamation, 10, 12

L
Lincoln, Abraham, 10

N
North, 8, 12
North America, 6

S
segregation, 18, 20
slave, 6, 10, 14, 18
slavery, 4, 6, 8, 16
South, 6, 8, 10, 12, 16

T
Texas, 12, 20

U
United States, 4, 8, 16, 20, 22

W
Washington, D.C., 22

WEBSITES

Due to the changing nature of Internet links, PowerKids Press has developed an online list of websites related to the subject of this book. This site is updated regularly. Please use this link to access the list: www.powerkidslinks.com/HH/juneteenth